DIGITAL AND INFORMATION LITERACY ™

SEARCHING ONLINE FOR IMAGE, AUDIO, AND VIDEO FILES

ADAM FURGANG

rosen publishing's
rosen
central®

New York

*For Benjamin and Caleb, may you always find
what you are searching for*

Published in 2010 by The Rosen Publishing Group, Inc.
29 East 21st Street, New York, NY 10010

Copyright © 2010 by The Rosen Publishing Group, Inc.

First Edition

Library of Congress Cataloging-in-Publication Data

Furgang, Adam.
Searching online for image, audio, and video files / Adam Furgang.—1st ed.
    p. cm.—(Digital and information literacy)
Includes bibliographical references and index.
ISBN-13: 978-1-4358-5318-8 (library binding)
1. Pictures—Computer network resources—Juvenile literature. 2. Sound recordings—Computer network resources—Juvenile literature. 3. Video recordings—Computer network resources—Juvenile literature. 4. Internet research—Juvenile literature. 5. Internet searching—Juvenile literature. 6. Electronic information resources literacy—Juvenile literature. I. Title.
ZA4675.F87 2010
025.0425—dc22

2008051726

Manufactured in Malaysia

CONTENTS

INTRODUCTION

Not long ago, students doing research for school reports had limited resources. They could use only printed information that came from books, magazines, newspapers, and encyclopedias. Not surprisingly, creating reports before the Internet took longer, and the final product did not always look very interesting. To spice up a school report and add some dramatic flair, students could paste in pictures taken from magazines they owned. Perhaps they could photocopy images from books at the public library. Any charts or graphs had to be created carefully by hand. And making audio or video presentations was even more difficult, requiring the borrowing of big, bulky audio-visual equipment from the school library's A.V. department. Why did students have to work this way? People did not have personal computers or the Internet in their homes, schools, or libraries.

Today, computers are part of our everyday life. Now it is common for students to use a personal computer, go online, and surf the Web to access all kinds of media, including image, audio, and video files. After a person finds these files, they can then be downloaded onto his or her computer. This means that these files can be transferred and copied from one computer system to another.

School reports can be fun and creative when using the Internet. It is now possible for students to make multimedia projects (projects that use more than

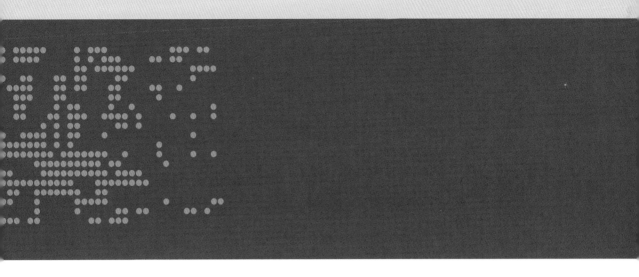

one form of communication and delivery of information). Students have many choices about how they can meet the requirements of a report. They can download image, audio, or video files to go with their reports. They can create a weblog, or "blog" as they are commonly known. Another choice for making a multimedia report is a podcast, which is a portable audio or video presentation.

Searching for image, audio, or video files on the Internet can be done quickly, but you must know how to get them from the right sources and how to save the files properly. Navigating the Internet can sometimes seem confusing. This book will help you to search for and save multimedia files that can be used in a school report. This book will not teach you how to download multimedia files illegally. It is important to know where and how to get the right information on the Internet. Many popular and well-respected Web sites do not allow people to download and copy files for their own use. However, most Internet files can still be used in an oral report. You simply need to give credit to the source in your bibliography and then present the file on a school computer as part of your classroom presentation.

Good Internet skills and habits can last you a lifetime. The best place to start is learning to use the Internet as a valuable research tool for school reports.

Chapter 1

Internet Research Basics

The Internet can be used like a resource library. But not everything in this cyberlibrary is reliable. You must question what you find on the Internet and use only reliable sources for school reports. Anyone can make a Web site and include any information on it, whether it is factually correct or not. Over time, you will become better able to decide which Web sites are reliable and which are not. Web sites with digital versions of previously published print information may be reliable. Other good research tools include the Library of Congress Web site, at http://www.loc.gov, and the Internet Public Library Web site, at http://www.ipl.org. When using Web sites that you are unsure about, double-check information you find to make sure that at least two other reliable Web sites list the same fact.

Web Browsers

There are two main types of personal computers that run different operating systems. An operating system is the basic software that supports a computer

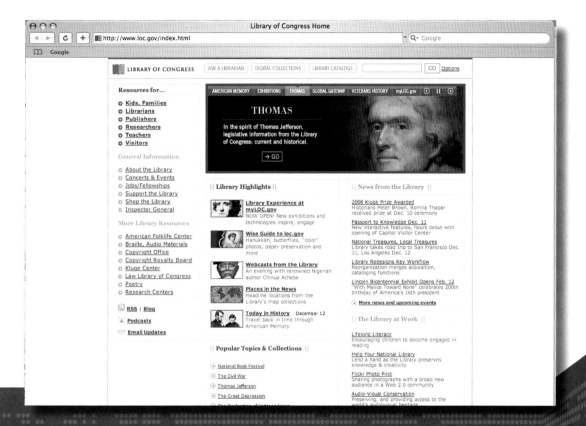

The Library of Congress Web site (http://www.loc.gov) is a reliable source—and incredibly rich resource—to use in school reports.

and makes it run. A computer known as a PC (stands for "personal computer") is one that runs a Microsoft Windows–based operating system. A Macintosh ("Mac") computer is one that runs an Apple operating system. There are some differences between these machines, but surfing the Internet is roughly the same for both kinds of computers.

Each type of computer has a Web browser that comes already installed on the computer when it is purchased. A Web browser is software that allows a computer connected to the Internet to see and navigate Web sites online. On Windows-based computers, the browser is Internet Explorer.

Blake Ross is the cocreator of Firefox, a free Internet browser that has become a popular method for surfing the Net. It can be downloaded for free for use on either a Mac or a PC.

On a Mac, the Web browser is Safari. Another popular Web browser that can be downloaded for free for either a Mac or PC is called Firefox.

Search Engines

Once you have accessed the Internet through a Web browser, you will be able to type a Web site address into the menu bar at the top of your screen. But you will not be able to make a broad search for a research topic for a report. Instead, you will need a good search engine to help you locate multiple sites covering the same topic.

A search engine is not actually an engine at all. It is a Web site that uses software that will locate documents that exist on millions of computers connected to the Internet. Good search engines sort information based on relevance to the topic, frequency of use by other computer users (popularity based on "hits," or visits to the site), and keywords that a user types into the search field.

The most popular search engine is Google. In fact, Google is so popular that many Web surfers now use the word as a verb. When referring to an Internet search, one might say, "I will Google that information" instead of "I will research that information on the Internet." Although Google is the most popular search engine, it is not the only one. You can take the basics of what you will learn here about Google and apply it to other search engines.

How to Use Google

The first step is to type "http://www.google.com" into your Web browser's address field. You may find that you only need to type "google.com" or "google" instead of the entire address.

Next, click your mouse on the search field under the word "Google," and type the topic you are going to be researching. For example, if you are researching humpback whales, then type both words "humpback" and "whales" in the search field. For a broader search that will give you more general information, just type "whales." Broader searches help locate

When using Google (http://www.google.com) and other search engines, the results are based on the keywords entered in the search screen, in this case "humpback whales."

more Web sites. A narrower search will bring up fewer Web sites on a more specific topic.

A Google search will provide a list of Web sites that are related to your search topic. Click on the site you want to see. When you're finished looking at this site, click the back arrow button at the top left corner of your Web browser to return to the results of your Google search.

A good trick for doing Google searches is to put several words you want to appear together in quotation marks. For example, if you wanted to find something specific about humpback whales, you might type "humpback whale feeding habits" in quotation marks. Your search results on Google will then show results for Web pages in which those exact words were found in that exact order.

Another good tip for Google searches is using the + and – keys. By typing "humpback whales" + "right whales," your results will feature Web sites that have information about both topics. This can be helpful when searching for more than one topic at a time and for finding single Web sites that include information on both.

The – key can be used to help you eliminate topics you do not wish to find. If you type "humpback whales" – "right whales" into the Google search field, your results will show Web sites that have the text "humpback whales," but will exclude any sites that contain references to "right whales." Experiment with both of these useful techniques as you do your research.

Bookmarks

An important habit to get into when doing online multimedia research is to save the addresses to the Web sites that you have found and that you feel may be useful for your project. This is called making a bookmark. Just as a bookmark in a printed book will help you easily find where you left off, a bookmark on your Web browser will help you to return quickly to Web pages you found that you would like to visit again.

When you locate a Web site that you would like to bookmark, go to the top of your screen or your Web browser and look for the bookmark tab. On Microsoft Internet Explorer, bookmarks are referred to as "favorites." Use this feature to help with the speed and ease of your research and to remind you where you got your multimedia files and information.

To learn more about copyright laws, visit the Library of Congress Web site (http://www.loc.gov) and search "copyright law."

Fair Use

Now you have found the information or multimedia files you are looking for from a reliable Web site, and you have double-checked the important facts. Does that mean it is alright to download the file for use in your report? Not necessarily.

Most printed and online materials have a copyright. A copyright is the legal right to publish and sell a work. If someone else wants to print, copy, or download the work, he or she needs permission from the person or company that owns the copyright. This copyright law helps to protect the rights of the person who created, published, and/or owns the work.

As a student, however, you may not have to worry too much about asking for permission to use material from the Internet in your school reports. Most of the projects you do for school will fall under the category of fair use. The term "fair use" is part of the United States copyright law. It states that material may be quoted exactly, without permission from the creator, as long as credit is given to the creator and the material used is reasonably short. Fair use applies to multimedia works as well as printed works.

Something else that students should be aware of is plagiarism. Plagiarism is when someone takes another person's concepts, work, or exact words and presents them as his or her own. Once your research is done and your source material is found for a report, you must put all the information together into your own words and present it in your own way. Also, take care to credit direct quotes and not to quote too often.

Just as you do with a report created from print sources, you must also include multimedia sources in a bibliography. A bibliography lists all of the sources that you used in a report. Proper credit should be given in a bibliography to any source used to create your report.

MYTHS & FACTS

MYTH Information found in books is always more reliable than information found online.

FACT While the Internet may have more unreliable information than printed books, it is still a very valuable resource, one where a researcher can find a lot of good and trustworthy information. People who surf the Web for factual information simply need to take a few precautions to ensure that the information they are getting is accurate and reliable.

MYTH Information and files that come from a Web site ending in ".com" are less reliable than Web sites ending in ".org."

FACT The ending ".com" means "commercial," and the ending ".org" means "organization." There are many commercial Web sites, such as news agencies and well-established companies, that have very trustworthy and well-maintained Web sites. Some small agencies with an ".org" ending on their Web site may not have the necessary staff to fact-check all of their information properly. Some organizations are advancing a specific political or social agenda, which may color the information they present. It is best to judge a Web site based on its reputation rather than its URL.

MYTH I cannot do Internet research without an adult monitoring me because I may come across inappropriate content.

FACT While you should always search for image, audio, or video files under the guidance of an adult, there are some search engines that are safe and approved for use by young students. Yahoo! Kids is a search engine made by Yahoo! that provides search results geared toward students.

14

Chapter 2

Searching for Image Files on the Internet

Whenever you surf the Internet, you probably come across many images. You may think of an image as a photograph, but drawings, graphs, charts, and maps are also types of images. Just as magazines and books have pictures to make the pages look more interesting, Web sites also have pictures to help decorate the page or communicate ideas and data. When searching for images for a school report, you will be looking for images that communicate ideas, news, data, statistics, history, and other kinds of graphic (visual) information to the viewer.

How to Search for Images Online

The quickest way to search online for images is to use a search engine such as Google. In fact, Google has its own section just for searching images. It is located on the Google home page at the top and directly next to the "Web" search button. When you click on the "images" button, you will be brought to the Google page for searching images only. Simply type into the

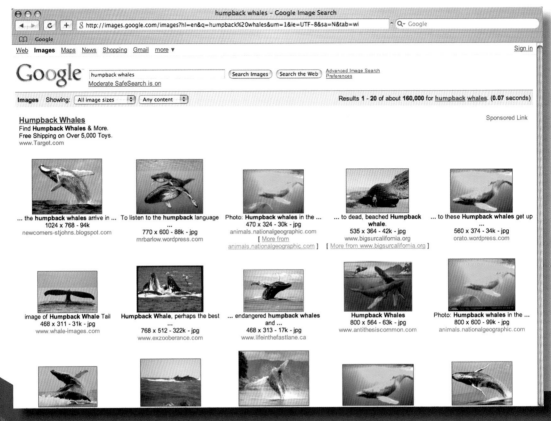

When doing searches on Google, you can navigate back and forth between searches of Web sites, images, and maps. Image results for a keyword search of "humpback whales" appear here.

search field the name or subject of the image you wish to search for, and Google will immediately list the results. Unlike the Web search, the results for an image search are displayed as many small pictures called thumbnails.

Picsearch is another search engine dedicated to finding photos online. It has a filter so that inappropriate images are blocked. Another way to find images online is to go to trusted Web sites that cover the topic you are trying to illustrate. For example, you can go to NASA's Web site for pictures of the space shuttle. However, most Web sites do not allow you to do keyword

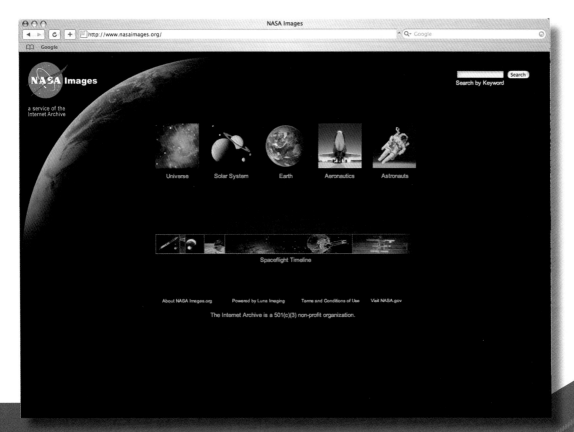

Web sites such as NASA.org are an excellent source for high-quality, well-documented photos. Government and public organization sites like NASA and the Library of Congress often feature public domain material, meaning they have no copyright and are free to use.

searches for photographs or other images. You must simply wander through the site for images that might match your search.

After looking through thumbnail images that have come up following a Google image search, you can focus in on a few images you might want to consider for your report. Each image found on Google Images will list the Web site where the image is actually located.

Once you click on the image, the search engine will then pull up a link to that Web page. This link contains the Web site's address, or URL. Think of

FILE TYPES

File Types

When you download images off the Internet, you will find that they may have different extensions, or ending letters. You may have seen files with names like canyon.jpeg or giraffe.gif. What do these letters mean? Files with ".jpeg" or ".gif" are generally used for images that originally appeared on Web sites. Other common file extensions for images are ".tiff" or ".png." Once you have downloaded an image from the Internet, test it to see if your computer can open it. You may have to choose another image if your computer cannot open certain file types.

it as similar to a phone number. Just as no two phone numbers are alike, no two URLs are alike either. Every file stored on the Web has its unique place, and its URL can help you get back there should you need to visit and examine it again. Remember that it is important to bookmark sites that you may want to return to later. Do not worry that you are making too many bookmarks. They can be deleted from your Web browser when your project is finished.

Using Reliable Sources

The next step to finding the right online images to use in a report is to focus only on the ones that come from reliable sources. Although you may find an image of what you are looking for in a matter of seconds, that does not mean that the image is suitable for use in your school report.

When searching online for images, do not always trust every caption and image description you see. The rules that apply to finding the most

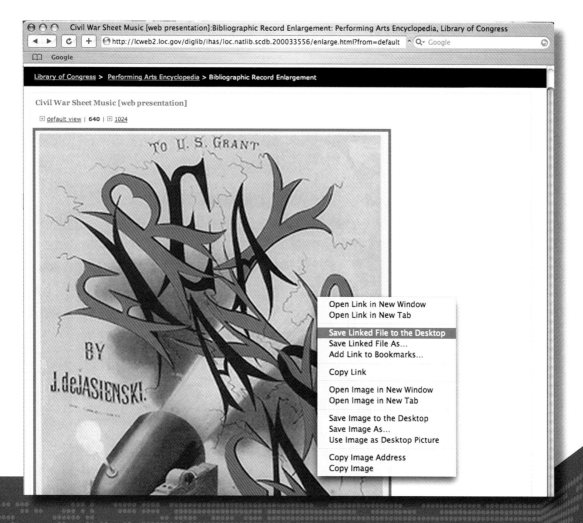

To save this image of Civil War–era sheet music from a Web site to the desktop of a PC, right-click and choose from the choices on the "save" menu.

reliable text from Web sites also apply to searching for images online. Use the most reliable and well-known sources first, then double-check your results against another Web site.

Suppose you have the choice between two good photos of a lowland gorilla. One comes from someone's vacation pictures on his or her personal Web site. The other comes from the National Geographic Web site. In this case, it is best to use the image that comes from National Geographic. The photo will most likely list the photographer's name and provide all of the other citation information that you will need to put into your bibliography. The source is highly reputable, and the image from National Geographic will probably have the most reliable caption information to help you identify the animal, its location, and the circumstances captured by the photo.

Saving Images Found on the Internet

Once you have found the images that you would like to download onto your computer, simply use your mouse to drag the image from the Web site onto your desktop. Remember to hold down the mouse button while dragging the image you want. Carefully place the image file in the particular folder or specific place on your desktop where you want to store it. Then release your finger from the mouse button. Double-check to be sure the image was successfully copied onto your desktop.

On a PC, you can also right-click on an image to bring up a menu on your screen. Select "copy" from the menu. Navigate to a new location or folder. Right-click again and select "paste" from the menu.

Having saved the file to your desktop, you can rename the image so that you will quickly recognize it when you need to call it up again. To do this, simply click on the file once to highlight it. Then click the image's filename and type in a new name. Choose something obvious that clearly describes the image contained in the file, like "VeroBeachPelicanInFlight." But be sure to keep the period at the end of the filename and the letters that appear after it. These letters are needed for your computer to recognize and read the file.

If you are saving a lot of images, renaming them all can waste time. It may help to use a simple photo-browsing program. Mac computers come with a program called iPhoto for organizing photos. PC computers often use a program from Google called Picasa, which can be downloaded for free.

Chapter 3

Searching for Audio Files on the Internet

n the past, sound was recorded on vinyl records (albums) or on magnetic tape. Today, digital sound recording is common. When you hear sound recordings online, you are hearing sound that was recorded digitally and posted to the Internet.

Why Use Audio?

When preparing and compiling a multimedia report, you have many choices. When you can use eye-catching and dynamic visual images such as pictures and video, you might wonder why someone would want to use audio-only files. Although most video files contain audio also, it is the video that may be more interesting for your audience to experience. However, sometimes audio may be the only thing available. Older speeches, radio broadcasts, and early recordings may be available only in an audio format, with no accompanying video. Many useful news broadcasts about the terrorist attacks of September 11, 2001, for example, were delivered by radio reporters and are only available in audio files.

Thomas Alva Edison was issued more than a thousand patents for his inventions. One of the most important and memorable ones was for sound recording technology and the phonograph machine. Here he listens to cylinder recordings played on a phonograph.

Sometimes, audio files are the perfect accompaniment to your subject matter. Suppose, for example, your multimedia report was on the birth of radio. In that case, using audio files might help to create an accurate and atmospheric mood of the era you are describing.

Before you begin your research, make sure your school has the resources you need to present a multimedia report. Some schools may not be able to play video downloaded from the Internet, for example. In that case, keep in mind that the audio can be taken from a video file and used on its own.

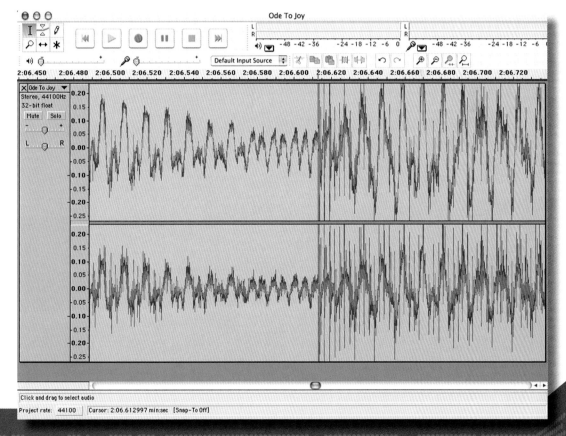

Sound recordings can be downloaded easily on a computer and tinkered with through the use of editing programs.

Finding Audio Files

You might wonder where you can find audio files on the Internet. Google does not currently have a specialized search engine for finding audio files. However, you can still use it to enter in a specific search for audio. Other search engines are dedicated to locating audio and video files. Sites such as altavista.com and audio.search.yahoo.com are among the most popular. Simply enter the sound, speech, or song you are looking for.

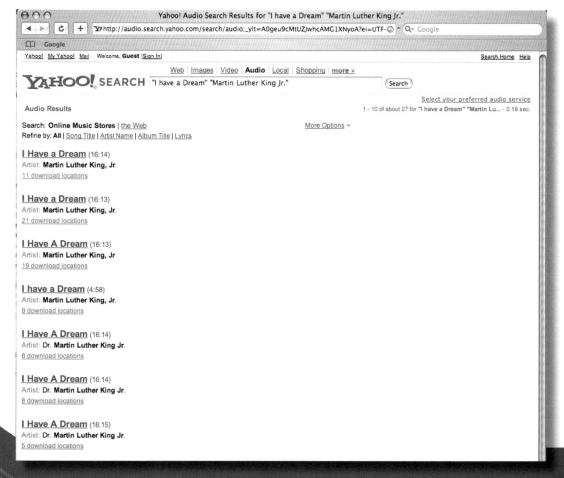

Yahoo.com is one of the most popular places to search for audio files, such as Dr. Martin Luther King Jr.'s landmark "I have a dream" speech.

For example, if you are looking for Dr. Martin Luther King Jr.'s famous "I have a dream" speech, simply enter it into the Yahoo! audio search field and click on "Audio Search." You will be given a list of search results, similar to the ones given in a Google search. Click on one of the links listed under "Results." You will be brought to a page that shows the download locations of that speech on the Internet. The search lists whether a download is available for a Mac or a PC, the file format you will be downloading, and the Internet browser that will be needed to do the download.

File   Edit   View   Favorites   Tools   Help

PLACES TO FIND AUDIO FILES

Places to Find Audio Files

Here are some search engines that specialize in finding audio and/or video files. After finding the files you want, follow the directions in this chapter or follow the search engine's own prompts to download them or listen to them from your computer.

http://www.altavista.com/audio
http://www.findsounds.com
http://audio.search.yahoo.com

Most important, the search also lists the price, if any, that the download will cost you. Do not download files that require you to pay a fee or subscribe to a site. For the purposes of a school report, it is best to look for free downloads only. If a free download is available, click on it and follow the instructions to save a copy of the file onto your desktop. If possible, listen to the file first before downloading it. This will help you to make sure it is the file you are looking for.

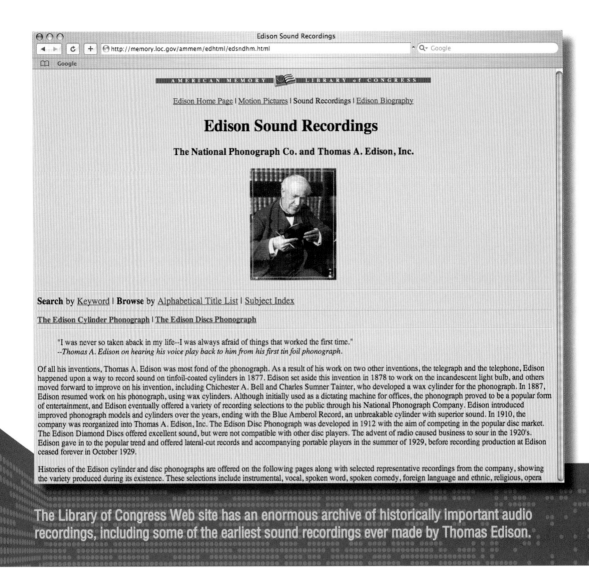

The Library of Congress Web site has an enormous archive of historically important audio recordings, including some of the earliest sound recordings ever made by Thomas Edison.

Other places on the Internet to find audio clips are major news organizations, library databases, collections, and archives. Web sites such as that of the United States Library of Congress have massive archives of information, including extensive audio collections. These same audio files may not be found nearly as easily when using a broader search engine like Google or Yahoo!.

Audio File Formats

Just as with image files, audio files have their own file names with their own extensions at the end, so you can recognize them easily. Some common extensions for audio files are "MP3," "AIFF," and "AC3." The most common audio file type today is the MP3.

MP3s have become the standard audio file format for copying audio CDs to personal home computers and also for downloading music from music-selling services like iTunes and Napster. The MP3 format is used in portable digital music players, which are commonly known as MP3 players. While searching online for audio clips, you are certain to come across these as well as other audio file formats.

Downloading and Saving Audio Files

Not all audio files appear to the computer user in the same way. You have to be able to recognize a file and how it is stored on the Internet for downloading and using. Unlike image files, many audio files are often listed simply as a URL to show you where on the Internet the sound can be found. Other times, you will see a file extension at the end of the filename, such as "audiofile.mp3" or "audiofile.aif." Still other times, you might see a filename and then a link to click on, such as: "Audio Speech File . . . Download." Seeing the word "download" in another color helps the user know where to click with the mouse to make the download occur.

When you click on a link to download a file, your computer will prompt you by asking where on your machine you would like to save the file. If you are just downloading one or two files, you may just choose your desktop as the file's download location. But be sure to keep track of files and keep them organized. Create folders to store files in, and name them so you can easily locate them when your research is finished.

Remember that not all files are allowed to be downloaded from the Internet. Many Web sites prevent downloading so that users do not steal files for illegal use. If a file is not allowed to be downloaded, you may still use it

Audio files—including music, speeches, and broadcasts—can be downloaded from a computer and stored on the computer itself or on an iPod or other MP3 player.

in your research and report. You may be able to give a multimedia report in a classroom with a computer that is connected to the Internet. Use a series of bookmarked links that quickly take you to the audio information you would like to present. Then provide the links in a written report to your teacher so that he or she can visit them at another time when your paper is being graded or reread.

Copyright and Fair Use with Audio Files

The copyright rules that apply to audio files are strict. Any sharing, downloading, or exchanging of copyrighted audio works is illegal. It is possible for someone today to share an entire music library of hundreds or even thousands of songs with someone else in just minutes. However, this should not be done. Downloading music or other copyrighted files off the Internet without permission or payment is illegal, even for purposes of research.

Let's say your topic is the antiwar and civil rights movements of the 1960s, and you wish to include a discussion of how these issues were reflected in the music of Bob Dylan. If you want your report to feature a few of his songs, you will have to pay to download them off the Internet. However, obtaining a song online usually costs less than a dollar. You can then be sure your music is obtained legally and can be included in your report. Another option would be to play a CD during the report or simply play the song from the Internet rather than downloading it. No matter what you decide to do, remember to give the appropriate credit to the artist and the music label the song was published under. Once a song has been downloaded from the Internet, you may use it for your own personal enjoyment, even after your multimedia report is finished.

Not all audio works are copyrighted. Some older works no longer have a copyright and may be downloaded for free. If you are unsure about which artists' works are copyrighted, try putting the artist's name in a search engine along with the word "copyright" to see if you can find any information about it.

How to Store and Play Back Audio Files

Once an audio file is downloaded and saved to your computer, deciding where to store it and how to listen to it are the next steps. When you listened to a file off the Internet, the music was being played through software that came from your Web browser. But now that the file is saved on your desktop, you may need a media player to play the file properly. A media player is a program that plays back audio or video files. Both a Macintosh and a Windows-based PC computer come with some kind of media player built in. Most PCs come with Microsoft Windows Media Player. Most Macs come with Apple's QuickTime Player or iTunes. Many other media players can be downloaded for free from the Internet.

Chapter 4

Searching for Video Files on the Internet

ideo is the most recent addition to the Internet. Over the years, computers have become more powerful and connections to the Internet have become faster. This has made it easier to upload and download large video clips from the Internet.

Today, in fact, anyone can easily upload (post) video clips to the Internet after filming footage with their cell phone, video camera, or webcam. This huge mass of often amateur online videos can make it difficult to find serious and substantial videos to use for research or for a multimedia report. A search online for tornado footage, for example, will bring you not only to footage shot by news agencies but also to videos shot by amateurs.

This may not be a bad thing, however. Video footage of news events captured by amateurs can be more striking than footage shot by a news agency. This is because someone who just happens to be at the right place at the right time has the opportunity to shoot the video. The professional photographer from the news agency is often not able to capture an unplanned event and be there in time to shoot it. Many news agencies have begun to recognize this. Cable News Network (CNN) has recently launched iReport,

Modern handheld video cameras and cell phones can easily record footage that can then be posted to the Internet or used in your multimedia presentation.

a section of its Web site dedicated to news, opinions, images, and videos provided by amateurs and regular citizens. Although the quality of an amateur video may not be as good as a professional's work, it may still be the most informative video available on a given subject.

There is a lot of valuable information on the Internet, but there is also a lot of junk. One of the greatest challenges for a student is to find what is

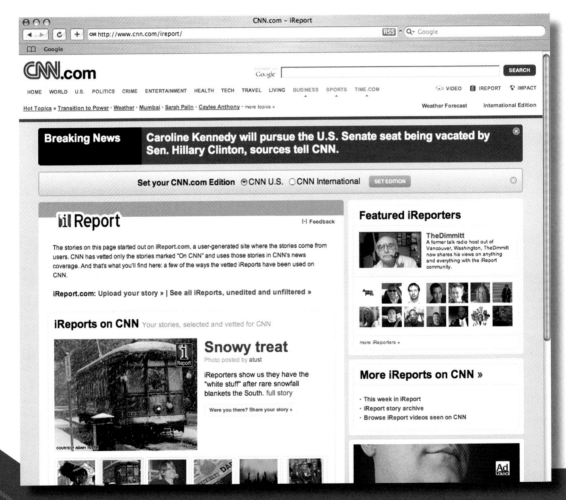

Amateur videos on a variety of topics are now featured on some reliable news and information Web sites. CNN.com posts videos captured by its viewers on a section of its Web site called iReport.

appropriate for a school report and ignore the inappropriate material that he or she may come across during online searches.

Finding Video Files

When looking for specialized videos on the Internet, it is sometimes worthwhile to skip search engines altogether and go directly to some trusted Web sites related to your research topic. For example, if you need video related to the space program, going directly to the NASA Web site would quickly provide you with the most reliable, relevant, and high-quality videos. Other sites

Many respected newspapers, like the *New York Times* (http://www.nytimes.com), have sections dedicated to video and podcasts created by their own reporters, videographers, and photographers.

with high-quality, substantial video include NOVA, the Library of Congress, CNN, and other reputable news agencies.

Sometimes, your research topic will require that you use a general search engine, however. The two most popular methods for finding video today on the Internet are YouTube.com and video.google.com. These sites may display search results by listing the most popular videos found under your subject category first. The first videos listed often feature pop culture approaches to the topic instead of information-rich educational or news-related treatments of the subject matter.

After getting search results for your research topic, click on one of the links to view the video. As you play it, adjust the volume on your computer

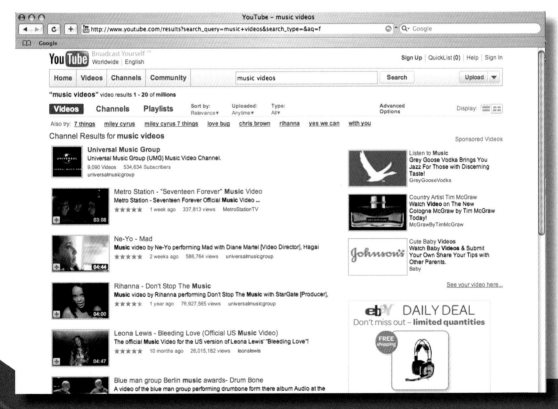

YouTube is one of the most popular places on the Internet to find videos, but its enormous number of unscholarly amateur videos may not always be helpful for school reports.

to make sure the sound is working properly. You will most likely see what is called streaming video. This means that you will see a play and a pause button at the bottom of the video. As you play the video, a tracking button will move across the bottom of the frame to show how much time is left before the video ends. This kind of streaming video cannot be downloaded to your computer. It can be viewed only on the Internet. If you want to use it in a presentation, you will have to have a computer with an Internet connection by your side so you can stream the video and show it to your audience. Be sure to credit your sources in your bibliography and bookmark the place where you found the video.

Using Streaming Video in a Presentation

Suppose you wanted to use a presidential speech in a school report. It is a streaming video, so you cannot download the video. After watching it, you realize that it is ten minutes long. The part you are interested in using, however, is only a thirty-second segment. What can you do? Find the part of the video you are interested in using and write down the time that appears at the bottom of the video screen. This time frame can be used as a marker to find the same place in the video each time you play it. When playing the video in class, you can move the cursor to the correct time frame and play the correct segment. This way you can quickly find the appropriate segment and show it to your audience, without forcing them to watch several minutes of irrelevant video before getting to the content that is important.

Podcasts

While streaming video cannot be downloaded from the Internet, video podcasts have been created for the purpose of being downloaded. Video podcasts are meant to be downloaded to an MP3 player for portable use. They can also be downloaded to your computer's hard drive. Check news sites for video podcasts related to your research topic. Remember to credit a podcast just as you would credit any other source in your bibliography.

TEN GREAT QUESTIONS

TO ASK A LIBRARIAN

1   How do I credit a Web site in my bibliography?

2   How long should an audio or video file take to download from the Internet?

3   How long should I keep my research stored on my computer after I hand in my report?

4   Is it possible for my computer to freeze as a result of downloading files from the Internet?

5   Should I write to the person who holds a copyright on an image, audio, or video file I want to use and ask for permission to use it in my report?

6   The rules of fair use say that I can use a small portion of a copyrighted work in my report if I credit the source. How short should the portion be?

7   Can downloading files from the Web give my computer a virus?

8   How can I be sure that an image I download from the Internet has not been altered?

9   How can I use the Internet to help me decide on a good topic for a multi-media report?

10   What should I do if I cannot find the information I am looking for online?

Downloading and Saving Video

How to download and save video files differs from Web site to Web site. If a file can be downloaded, it will usually have a button or a highlighted text link to click in order to begin the download process. Sometimes, the file format name as well as its size will be listed. This is helpful information that lets you know if the file is in a format your computer can use and if its size is too big for your computer's storage capacity.

Remember to save files to a specific location on your computer so that you can easily locate them again later. Also remember to rename files so you

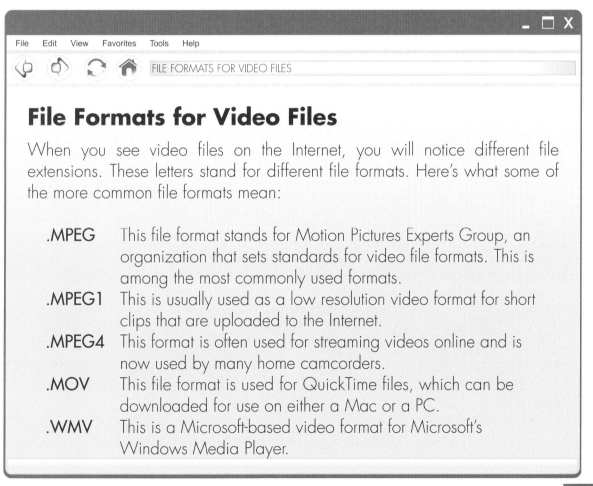

FILE FORMATS FOR VIDEO FILES

File Formats for Video Files

When you see video files on the Internet, you will notice different file extensions. These letters stand for different file formats. Here's what some of the more common file formats mean:

.MPEG   This file format stands for Motion Pictures Experts Group, an organization that sets standards for video file formats. This is among the most commonly used formats.

.MPEG1   This is usually used as a low resolution video format for short clips that are uploaded to the Internet.

.MPEG4   This format is often used for streaming videos online and is now used by many home camcorders.

.MOV   This file format is used for QuickTime files, which can be downloaded for use on either a Mac or a PC.

.WMV   This is a Microsoft-based video format for Microsoft's Windows Media Player.

will know what they are. Many files on the Internet can have odd names with nothing more than a string of letters and numbers that will give you no clue about what the file actually contains. When you rename a file, be sure to keep the extension letters at the end of the filename so that your computer can recognize the file format the file is saved in. For example, you might download a file from the Internet of an automobile assembly line in action. The file name might be something like "jhsgdjs235276526.MP4." It would make sense for you to rename the file something like "assembly_line_01.MP4."

Always check the size and format of a file before trying to download it onto your computer. The file may be too large for your computer's memory capacity or may be in a format that your computer doesn't recognize and can't open or read.

You saved the MP4 format extension for your computer to recognize, and you named the file 01 at the end so that you can tell it apart from other videos you download on the same topic.

Pulling It Together

Having learned how to search for, download, save, and retrieve image, audio, and video files from the Internet, you are now ready to pull all of these multimedia elements together into a single, dynamic presentation. As with any large research project, you may end up with more material than you can use. Resist the temptation to throw every piece of multimedia research you've found into the report. Just like when you edit printed research materials and include only those sources that are relevant to your subject and illustrate your argument, so too should you whittle away your multimedia material until only the most essential and impactful elements remain. This will make your presentation or report tighter, more concise, more fluid, more effective, and more powerful. It's a brave new world of online research. Get out there and enjoy it!

GLOSSARY

blog From the term "weblog," meaning a Web site of journal or log entries.

bookmark The electronic saving, or marking, of a Web site so that the user can return to it easily at a later time.

copyright The legal right to publish and sell a work.

download To transfer and copy digital information from one computer to another.

extension Letters appearing after a period at the end of a filename, indicating the specific file format.

fair use The part of the United States copyright law that says that material may be quoted exactly, without permission from the creator, as long as credit is given to the creator and the material used is reasonably short.

file format The way digital information is saved and stored on a computer, usually indicated by letters at the end of the filename.

hard drive The place where all of a computer's files and software are stored.

Internet The virtual network connecting millions of computers worldwide.

media player A program or device that plays back audio or video files.

multimedia The use of more than one form of communication, such as image, audio, or video files.

plagiarism The act of taking another person's concepts, work, or exact words and presenting it as your own, without citing the original work or giving proper credit to its author/creator.

podcast Digital media file that is distributed over the Internet for use on portable media or MP3 players.

search engine A Web site that uses software designed to locate documents that exist on millions of computers connected to the Internet.

URL The address of a Web site.

Web browser Software that allows a computer connected to the Internet to see and navigate Web sites online.

Childnet International
Studio 14 Brockley Cross Business Centre
96 Endwell Road
London SE4 2PD
England
Web site: http://childnet-int.org
Childnet International works to help make the Internet a safe place for children.

Computers for Youth
322 Eighth Avenue, Floor 12A
New York, NY 10001
(212) 563-7300
Web site: http://www.cfy.org
Computers for Youth provides inner-city students with home computers and
    provides training and technical support so that students can do better
    in school.

The Copyright Society of the U.S.A.
352 Seventh Avenue, Suite 739
New York, NY 10001
Web site: http://www.copyrightkids.org
Copyright Kids is a part of the Copyright Society of the U.S.A. It offers
    information about various copyrighted online media.

Get Net Wise
Internet Education Foundation
1634 I Street NW
Washington DC 20009
Web site: http://www.getnetwise.org

Get Net Wise is part of the Internet Education Foundation, which works to provide a safe online environment for children and families.

Just Think
39 Mesa Street, Suite 106
San Francisco, CA 94129
(415) 561-2900
Web site: http://justthink.org
Just Think is a nonprofit foundation that promotes media literacy for young people.

Media Awareness Network
1500 Merivale Road, 3rd Floor
Ottawa, ON K2E6Z5
Canada
(613) 224-7721
Web site: http://www.media-awareness.ca
The Media Awareness Network creates media literacy programs for young people. The site contains educational games about the Internet and media.

Web Sites

Due to the changing nature of Internet links, Rosen Publishing has developed an online list of Web sites related to the subject of this book. This site is updated regularly. Please use this link to access this list:

http://www.rosenlinks.com/dil/iavf

Fahs, Chad. *How to Do Everything with YouTube*. New York, NY: The McGraw-Hill Companies, 2008.

Gaines, Ann. *Ace Your Internet Research* (Ace It! Information Literacy). Berkeley Heights, NJ: Enslow Publishers, 2009.

Gosney, John W. *Blogging for Teens*. Florence, KY: Course Technology PTR, 2004.

Haag, Tim, and Dona Herweck Rice. *Internet for Kids*. Westminster, CA: Teacher Created Resources, 2005.

Hock, Randolph. *The Extreme Searcher's Internet Handbook*. 2nd ed. Medford, NJ: CyberAge Books, 2007.

Lester, James, Sr., and James Lester Jr. *Research Paper Handbook*. 3rd ed. Tuscon, AZ: Good Year Books, 2005.

Roza, Greg. *The Incredible Story of Computers and the Internet* (Kid's Guide to Incredible Technology). New York, NY: PowerKids Press, 2004.

Sorenson, Sharon. *A Quick Reference to Internet Research*. New York, NY: Amsco School Publishing Inc., 2004.

Taylor, Allan, and James Robert Parish. *Career Opportunities in the Internet, Video Games, and Multimedia*. New York, NY: Checkmark Books, 2007.

BIBLIOGRAPHY

Busby, Michael. *Learn Google*. Plano, TX: Wordware Publishing, Inc., 2004.

Fahs, Chad. *How to Do Everything with YouTube*. New York, NY: The McGraw-Hill Companies, 2008.

Graves, Ralph. "Digital Audio/Video File Formats: The Basics." Crutchfield.com, April 9, 2008. Retrieved September 2008 (http://www.crutchfield.com/learn/learningcenter/home/fileformats.html).

Graves, Ralph. "File Formats Library." Crutchfield.com, April 19, 2008. Retrieved September 2008 (http://www.crutchfield.com/learn/learningcenter/home/fileformats_glossary.html).

Hock, Randolph. *The Extreme Searcher's Internet Handbook*. 2nd ed. Medford, NJ: CyberAge Books, 2007.

Komando, Kim. "Web Search Engines Make Finding Audio Files Easy." *USA Today*, September 4, 2005. Retrieved October 2008 (http://www.usatoday.com/tech/columnist/kimkomando/2005-09-04-audio-searches_x.htm).

Library of Congress. "Sonic: How to Search." Retrieved August 2008 (http://www.loc.gov/rr/record/Sonichow.html).

Liethen Kunka, Jennifer, and Joe Barbato. "MLA Formatting and Style Guide Works Cited: Electronic Sources." The Owl at Purdue. Retrieved September 2008 (http://owl.english.purdue.edu/owl/resource/557/09/).

Nizza, Mike, and Patrick Witty. "In an Iranian Image, a Missile Too Many." *New York Times*, July 10, 2008. Retrieved July 2008 (http://thelede.blogs.nytimes.com/2008/07/10/in-an-iranian-image-a-missile-too-many/index.html?hp).

Pederson, Ted, and Francis Moss. *Internet for Kids*. New York, NY: Price Stern Sloan, 2001.

Shaw, Maura D. *Mastering Online Research*. Cincinnati, OH: Writer's Digest Books, 2007.

University of Texas System. "CONFU: The Conference on Fair Use."
    Retrieved August 2008 (http://www.utsystem.edu/ogc/
    intellectualproperty/confu.htm).
University of Texas System. "Fair Use Guidelines for Educational Multimedia."
    Retrieved August 2008 (http://www.utsystem.edu/ogc/
    intellectualproperty/ccmcguid.htm).
Walker, Janice R., and Todd Taylor. *The Columbia Guide to Online Style.*
    New York, NY: Columbia University Press, 2006.

INDEX

About the Author

Adam Furgang is an artist and graphic designer who has spent a lot of time searching online for image, audio, and video files to use in his various art and design projects. He has used many search engines and graphics programs to search, download, and manipulate media. He has written several books for Rosen Central about topics such as technology, the environment, and transportation.

Photo Credits

Cover, p. 1 (left), p. 28 © Martin Ruetschi/Keystone/Corbis; cover, p. 1 (second from left), p. 31 © Solus-Veer/Corbis; cover, p. 1 (second from right), p. 22 National Park Service, Edison National Historic Site; cover, p. 1 (right) © www.istockphoto.com/fotek; p. 8 © AP Images; p. 38 © David Grossman/The Image Works.

Designer: Nicole Russo; Photo Researcher: Cindy Reiman